THE CHANGING CLIMATE OF

EUROPE

Patricia K. Kummer

Cavendish Square
New York

Published in 2014 by Cavendish Square Publishing, LLC
303 Park Avenue South, Suite 1247, New York, NY 10010

First Edition

Website: cavendishsq.com

CPSIA Compliance Information: Batch #WW14CSQ

All websites were available and accurate when this book was sent to press.

Library of Congress Cataloging-in-Publication Data
Kummer, Patricia K.
The changing climate of Europe / by Patricia K. Kummer.
p. cm. — (Climates and continents)
Includes index.
ISBN 978-1-62712-449-2 (hardcover) ISBN 978-1-62712-450-8 (paperback) ISBN 978-1-62712-451-5 (ebook)
1. Climatic changes — Environmental aspects — Europe. I. Kummer, Patricia K. II. Title.
QC903.2.E85 K86 2014
363.738—dc23

Editorial Director: Dean Miller
Senior Editor: Peter Mavrikis
Copy Editor: Cynthia Roby
Art Director: Jeffrey Talbot
Designer: Amy Greenan
Photo Researcher: Alison Morretta
Production Manager: Jennifer Ryder-Talbot
Production Editor: Andrew Coddington

Expert Reader: Victor Savage, associate professor, Department of Geography, National University of Singapore

The photographs in this book are used by permission and through the courtesy of: Cover photo by Image Source/Image Source/Getty Images, Davor Pukljak/Shutterstock.com; Davor Pukljak/Shutterstock.com, 4; Mapping Specialists, 6; Simon Greenwood/Lonely Planet Images/Getty Images, 8; Dorling Kindersley/Getty Images, 9; Antonio Zanghì/Flickr/Getty Images, 10; David Gould/The Image Bank/Getty Images, 11; Angelo Cavalli/Robert Harding World Imagery/Getty Images, 12; Mapping Specialists, 13; Wade Eakle/Lonely Planet Images/Getty Images, 14; Minden Pictures/SuperStock. 16; Hiroshi Higuchi/Photolibrary/Getty Images, 18; Heinz Wohner/LOOK/Getty Images, 19; Ron Koeberer/Aurora/Getty Images, 21; Ragnar Th. Sigurdsson/age fotostock/SuperStock, 22; Sebastien Hreblay/Stringer/AFP/Getty Images, 23; Lee Frost/Robert Harding World Imagery/Getty Images, 24; AFP/Stringer/AFP/Getty Images, 25; Kim Walker/Robert Harding World Imagery/Getty Images, 26; Robert Harding Picture Library/SuperStock, 27; Jim Richardson/National Geographic/SuperStock, 28; DEA/G. CAPPELLI/Contributor/De Agostini/Getty images, 30; Adam Jones/Oxford Scientific/Getty Images, 31; Biosphoto/SuperStock, 32; Angelo Cavalli / SuperStock, 34; Nadia Isakova/AWL Images/Getty Images, 35; Alison Wright/National Geographic/Getty Images, 35; Nadia Isakova/AWL Images/Getty Images, 35; David Clapp/Oxford Scientific/Getty Images, 36; SEUX Paule/hemis.fr/hemis.fr/Getty Images, 37; Peter Adams/Photolibrary/Getty Images, 38; Hans-Peter Merten/The Image Bank/Getty Images, 40; Eye Ubiquitous/SuperStock, 41.

Printed in the United States of America

CONTENTS

ONE

THE PENINSULA CONTINENT

Looking at a globe or at a world map, it is quite easy to identify the seven **continents**. They are Earth's largest land areas. Europe is the second smallest of the seven continents. It covers only 7 percent of Earth's land area. The other six continents in order of size are Asia, Africa, North America, South America, Antarctica, and Australia.

Getting To Know Europe

If you look at the map on page 4, you can see why Europe is called a peninsula. It is surrounded by water on three sides. The Arctic Ocean is to the north. The Atlantic Ocean lies to the west. To the south, the Strait of Gibraltar and Mediterranean Sea separate Europe from Africa. To the southeast, the Aegean Sea, Dardanelles, Sea of Marmara, Bosporus Strait, and Black Sea separate Europe from Asia. To the east

The peninsular shape of Europe is seen in this photo taken from space. Europe's land is covered by forests and grasslands (green), dry lands (orange), snow and ice (white), and wetlands (light blue).

POLITICAL MAP OF EUROPE

Where in the World Is Europe?

Use the political map on page 6 to answer the following questions about the continent of Europe:

1. Which region of Europe and which country are closest to part of North America?
2. Which regions of Europe have countries that are partly in Asia? Name the countries.
3. Which regions of Europe are bordered by three other regions?
4. Which region of Europe and which country are closest to Africa?
5. Which country is made up of four separate areas? Name the areas.
6. Which country has the largest amount of land in Europe?

ANSWERS:

1. Northern Europe; Iceland
2. Eastern Europe, Southern Europe; Azerbaijan, Georgia, Kazakhstan, Russia, Turkey
3. Eastern Europe and Western Europe
4. Southern Europe; Spain
5. United Kingdom; England, Scotland, Wales, Northern Ireland
6. Russia

Part of a Basque wedding party in Navarra, Spain.

and southeast, the Ural Mountains, Ural River, Caspian Sea, and Caucasus Mountains also form Europe's boundary with Asia.

Besides being a peninsula, Europe is also made up of five peninsulas. Twenty-two of Europe's forty-nine countries are located on them. Norway and Sweden are on the Scandinavian Peninsula. Denmark and a small part of Germany are on the Jutland Peninsula. The Iberian Peninsula has Andorra, Portugal, and Spain. Italy, San Marino, and Vatican City make up the Apennine Peninsula. Albania, Bosnia-Herzegovina, Bulgaria, Croatia, European Turkey, Greece, Kosovo, Macedonia, Montenegro, Romania, Serbia, and Slovenia make up the Balkan Peninsula.

Europe's landmass is often divided into four regions—Northern, Eastern, Southern, and Western Europe. Each region has unique climate, land, or population features. For example, Southern Europe is made up of peninsulas and has a warm Mediterranean climate.

Europe's location gives the continent a variety of climate zones—

from the bitter-cold Arctic to the warm, wet Mediterranean. In turn, Europe's climates and landforms provide **habitats** for many plants and animals.

Although Europe covers the second-smallest land area, it has the world's third-largest population. Europe's people belong to about 87 ethnic groups. Each group shares the same language and culture and lives in specific areas. The Basque of Southern and Western Europe, the Sami of Northern Europe, and the Romani and Tatar of Eastern Europe are a few of Europe's small ethnic groups.

The Continents and Change

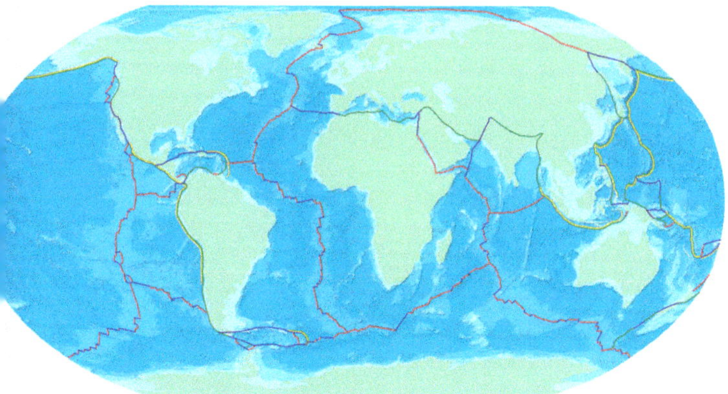

Earth's crust is made up of tectonic plates. Europe shares the Eurasian Plate with the continent of Asia.

For hundreds of millions of years, Europe and the other continents have undergone slow, continuous change. In fact, about 250 million years ago, there was only one continent—Pangaea. Gradually, Pangaea broke apart, and the seven continents that we know were formed. About 5 million years ago, Europe achieved the shape that it has today.

Because Earth's crust is made up of many **tectonic plates**, its surface and continents continue to change. These hard, rigid sheets of solid rock are always moving. Tectonic movement builds mountains and volcanoes. It also causes earthquakes and

Mount Etna

FIELD TRIP EXPLORATION

Mount Etna stands on Italy's island of Sicily. This mountain is Europe's largest and highest active volcano. With each eruption, Mount Etna changes height.

Scientists and historians have recorded Etna's eruptions since 1500 BCE. Those records have been kept longer than records for any other volcano in the world. They help volcanologists better understand the causes of eruptions.

Eruptions happen at Mount Etna because one of Earth's tectonic plates continues to slip farther under another one. Since 1999, Mount Etna has erupted at least once every year. Several eruptions occurred in 2013. Lava flowed down the mountain, and ash spewed over nearby land. Sometimes this volcano erupts from one of its sides and from the top at the same time.

Near the base of the mountain, crops grow in the fertile volcanic soil. Beech, birch, oak, and pine trees cover Mount Etna's slopes. Snow caps the summit much of the year.

volcanic eruptions. Europe continues to experience those natural disasters.

The United Kingdom is gradually closing its coal-fired power stations.

Another change that concerns Europe and the other continents is **climate change**. The main cause of climate change is the release of large amounts of carbon dioxide (CO_2) into the air. Natural events, such as volcanic eruptions, and human actions add to the amount of CO_2. The rise in CO_2 in the air is traced to Europe during the Industrial Revolution. In the 1800s, Europeans began burning large amounts of coal to run the machines in their factories. Burning of coal continues today, as well as burning of oil, natural gas, and gasoline. All of those fuels give off CO_2.

Europeans also contributed to climate change by altering their natural environment. They cut down large areas of forests, which absorb CO_2. In their place, they planted crops, dug mines, and built cities. Those actions increased the amount of CO_2 in the air, bringing warmer temperatures and varying rainfall. Now, Europe's leaders and people are working to improve the environment. Their actions are still bringing more changes to Europe.

TWO

MOUNTAINS, A GREAT PLAIN, WATERWAYS

Europe is famous for its snowcapped Alps and fertile Great European Plain. Some of its longest rivers are the Danube, Rhine, and Volga. Lakes Como, Geneva, and Ladoga are a few of its largest lakes. Bays, fjords, gulfs, and seas create Europe's 55,302 miles (89,000 km) of coastline.

Forests and grasses grow on the lower slopes of the Matterhorn, a high peak in the Swiss Alps.

PHYSICAL MAP OF EUROPE

Mount Elbrus, located in western Russia, is a dormant volcano that last erupted about 2,000 years ago.

Old and Young Mountains

Mountain ranges rise above each region of Europe. Northern Europe has the continent's oldest range—the Caledonia Mountains. They were formed about 400 million years ago. Tectonic plate movement causes these mountains to rise a tiny bit each year. Large deposits of coal are mined in the southern Caledonias.

In Eastern Europe, the Ural Mountains run north to south. They form part of Europe's boundary with Asia. The Urals were formed about 300 million years ago when the land that is now Europe slammed into Asia. Erosion from wind and water continue to wear them down. Large deposits of copper, iron ore, platinum, and zinc lie in the southern Urals.

Several mountain ranges extend across Southern Europe into Eastern Europe. All of these ranges were formed by tectonic plate movement between 10 and 60 million years ago. From west to east, the ranges include the Sierra Nevada, Pyrenees, Vosges, Alps, Apennines, Carpathians, and Caucasus. Mount Elbrus, located in Russia's Caucasus

Mountains, is Europe's highest point at 18,510 feet (5,642 m) above sea level. The Alps rise about 1/50 of an inch (0.5 mm) each year. They do not actually get taller, though. Erosion from wind, water, and the movement of **glaciers** wears them down at the same rate at which they grow. Dairy cows, goats, and sheep graze on the mountains' grassy slopes.

Plateaus and Highlands

Plateaus and other highlands border the mountain ranges. Rich soil for growing crops is found in highland river valleys. Forests, such as Germany's Black Forest, also cover much of the area. Deposits of coal, copper, and iron ore lie under the ground.

Deforestation has occurred in several places, though. **Open-pit mines** have replaced the trees. From those mines, large amounts of minerals have been taken from the ground. In dry areas, deforestation and open-pit mining have resulted in **desertification**. In some parts of Southern and Eastern Europe, the soil has become weak. It no longer supports crops, grasses, or trees. Plus, the soil washes away during rainstorms.

The Great European Plain

Europe's largest land region is the Great European Plain. It extends from southern France to the Ural Mountains. The southern United Kingdom is also part of this vast plain. Europe's plain has the continent's richest soil. Large fields of barley, corn, oats, potatoes, rye, sugar beets, and wheat cover the land. Many of those crops grow in the plain's wide river valleys.

Others grow on the plain's **steppe** in Eastern Europe. Cattle and sheep graze on the steppe's grasses. Deposits of coal, iron ore, natural gas, and petroleum lie under the plain. Some of Europe's largest cities, such as Berlin, Germany, and Warsaw, Poland, rise up on the plain.

The Netherland's Loonse and Drunese Dunes formed after deforestation and overgrazing in the 1300s.

As it happened in the highlands, deforestation and open-pit mining have also occurred in parts of Europe's plain. In addition, some of the plain's grassy steppe has been plowed under to grow crops. All of those actions have led to erosion and desertification on some parts of the plain.

Rivers, Lakes, and Coastlines

Many of Europe's rivers begin in the mountains. The Danube, Po, Rhine, and Rhone rivers flow from the Alps. Europe's longest river is the Volga. It runs 2,293 miles (3,689 km) through Russia and into the Caspian Sea. Before Europe's rivers empty into a sea or ocean, some form a delta (a wide triangle of land). The rich, watery soil on the Rhone and Volga deltas supports rice farming.

Getting the Lay of the Land

Study the physical map of Europe on page 13 to answer the following questions:

1. What six major rivers cross Europe's steppes?
2. Why do you think that Lakes Como, Constance, and Geneva are in the Alps?
3. Which two mountain ranges separate Europe from Asia?
4. Between which two mountain ranges does the Po River flow?
5. What is the main elevation of the Black Forest; of the Bialowieza Forest?

ANSWERS:

1. Danube, Dniester, Don, Dnieper, Volga, Ural
2. They were formed by melting snow from the mountains.
3. Urals, Caucasus
4. Alps, Apennines
5. 2,001 to 5,000 feet; 0 to 1,000 feet.

Europe's rivers often flood because of heavy rain or melting snow. Floodwaters deposit rich soil in the river valleys. But floods can also damage crops and farmland. Rivers also flood Europe's towns and large cities. Those floodwaters also fill streets and basements. To prevent floods, hundreds of dams have been built on Europe's rivers. The dams also produce hydroelectric power for Europe's farms, towns, and cities.

Europe is dotted with thousands of freshwater lakes. Finland alone has about 60,000 of them. Lake Ladoga in northwestern Russia is Europe's largest freshwater lake. Other large lakes, such as Lakes Como, Constance, Geneva, and Lucerne, are in the Alps. Europe shares the world's largest lake—the Caspian Sea—with Asia. It is actually a saltwater lake. Europe's lowest point—92 feet (28 m) below sea level—lies in Russia's part of the Caspian Sea.

Although Europe is a small continent, it has a long coastline. Deep bays, gulfs, and harbors cut into its coastal lands. Along Norway's western coast, glaciers dug fjords (deep inlets) from the mountains. Seawater filled the fjords. Today, the action of wind and water on the Baltic Sea has eroded large parts of that coastline. Dams on Europe's rivers have also caused coastal erosion. Along with water, the dams hold back sand and soil. Coastlines need the sand and soil to maintain their size and shape.

FIELD TRIP EXPLORATION

The Rhine River

After the Volga and the Danube, the Rhine is Europe's third-longest river. It flows from the Swiss Alps to the Rhine delta in The Netherlands and then into the North Sea. Canals connect the Rhine to the Danube and Rhone rivers. Barges move freight from cities along the river to ports on the North Sea. Passenger ships carry thousands of travelers who enjoy sights along the Rhine. All of that traffic make the Rhine Europe's busiest river.

Views along the Rhine include the Vosges Mountains to the west and the Black Forest to the east. Castles appear atop high hills around bends in the river. Scenic but busy cities such as Cologne and Dusseldorf stand along the Rhine.

THREE

WARMING TEMPERATURES, VARYING RAINFALL

Europe has a variety of climate zones. They range from the dry, bitter-cold Arctic to the warm Mediterranean. Europe's most extreme temperatures have been 118.4°F (47.9°C) in Athens, Greece, and -72.6°F (-58°C) in Ust'-Shchugor, Russia. Europe's annual precipitation (rain and snow) extremes are 183 inches (465 cm) in Crkvica, Bosnia-Herzegovina, and 6.4 inches (16 cm) in Astrakhan, Russia.

Yet, most of Europe enjoys a mild climate because of warm ocean currents. The Gulf Stream brings warm water from the Gulf of Mexico to the North Sea and North Atlantic. Strong winds blow from the west over that water. The winds warm the land and bring rain. They also stop cold Arctic winds from freezing Europe's coastlands in the winter. All of those conditions warm Europe's temperatures about 9°F (5°C).

Climate Change in Europe

Major differences in temperatures and precipitation over several years are known as climate change. Acts of nature and people cause climate change. In Europe, people have been responsible for most of the continent's climate change. Through hundreds of years, Europeans changed the use of their land. They cut down forests and plowed up grasslands to plant crops. Changes made to forests and grasslands affect the climate. Temperatures increase and rainfall decreases.

Europeans also built many of the world's largest cities, such as London and Paris. They covered land with houses, apartments, factories, and office buildings. They paved roads and streets with concrete and asphalt. All those actions created heat islands. Europe's cities can be as much as 9°F (5°C) warmer than nearby rural areas. This temperature difference comes from the heat given off by

The urban area of Paris, the capital of France, covers about 890 square miles (2,300 sq km) of land.

How Scientists Measure Climate Change

Scientists use many methods to measure climate change. Throughout Europe, they use regular thermometers and rain gauges at weather stations to record changes in daily and annual weather. They also study growth rings from trees. The rings tell when rainy and dry periods occurred during the past several hundred years. In Europe's Arctic, scientists study ice cores. The cores show that the past 100 years have been the warmest since 1600.

Other scientists observe and record changes in plant and animal behavior. For example, flowers and trees are budding earlier each spring. Leaves are changing color later in the fall. Some species of birds are returning north earlier each year. Many butterflies, birds, and mammals have moved to higher and cooler habitats in the Alps and on the tundra. All of those activities indicate warming temperatures.

A scientist examines an ice core near the Vatnajokull ice cap in Iceland.

a city's buildings, cars, buses, trains, trucks, and roadways.

In addition, Europe's homes, apartments, factories, and office buildings must be cooled and heated. Air conditioning requires **chlorofluorocarbons**. Large amounts of coal, oil, and natural gas are burned for heat and for cooking. In the past 50 years, the number of gasoline-powered cars in Europe has increased. Before that, most Europeans used public transportation—such as trains, trolleys, and buses. Those coolants and fuels give off CO_2 and other gases that add to climate change.

Results of Climate Change

During the past 100 years, Europe has experienced climate change. Overall, temperatures have become warmer by 1.3°F (0.74°C) throughout the continent. That is slightly more than the world's average increase of 1°F (0.6°C). Since 2000, Europe has experienced more and longer heat waves. This has caused at least 38,000 deaths—most of them in Europe's cities.

Europe's precipitation has changed, too. Heavier rains in parts of Northern and Eastern Europe have caused damaging floods. Less rainfall in other parts of Eastern Europe and in Southern Europe has led to **drought** and forest fires.

In dry areas of Europe, forest fires destroy large numbers of trees each year.

Throughout Europe, the warming climate has affected the environment. In the Arctic Ocean, both the amount of ice and depth of the ice have decreased. From the Pyrenees to the Caucasus, glaciers atop mountains are melting at faster rates. Warmer ocean waters have led to a rise in sea level. That in turn has caused flooding and erosion along Europe's coastlands. The Netherlands could suffer much damage from flooding. Parts of that country are already below sea level.

Ash spews into the sky during a volcanic eruption in Iceland.

Natural Disasters

Europe's main weather-related natural disasters are floods, heat waves, forest fires, and blizzards. Blizzards are powerful windstorms with heavy snowfall and freezing temperatures. They sometimes hit parts of Eastern Europe. All of those disasters cause human deaths and property damage.

Parts of Europe also experience natural disasters caused by tectonic plate movement. Earthquakes and volcanic eruptions take place mainly in Iceland and Southern Europe. Earthquakes sometimes shake hilly areas near the Mediterranean Sea. In 2012, Northern Italy experienced two damaging quakes within a few days. Entire towns became heaps of rubble. About 20,000 people were left homeless and another 23 were killed.

Europe has nine active volcanoes. Four of them are in Iceland. In

Cloudburst over Copenhagen

Copenhagen is the capital of Denmark. It sits on an island in the Baltic Sea. The city is famous for its castles, museums, and 160-year-old amusement park. The Tivoli Gardens has exciting rides, carnival games, and food tents. In addition, Tivoli is lined with trees, flower gardens, and fountains. Even at an amusement park, the people of Copenhagen appreciate nature.

Copenhagen has many examples of how people are protecting the environment. Near Copenhagen's airport, wind turbines generate much of the city's electricity. Many residents ride bicycles to work and to school. A clean, quiet rail system moves other people from place to place.

The city is also working to improve flood control. In two hours on July 2, 2011, Copenhagen received at least 6 inches (15 cm) of rain. During this cloudburst, streets and basements quickly flooded. Cars were underwater. By the end of 2011, the city had developed The Cloudburst Plan. Through the plan, rainwater will be channeled to the sea, parks, and open spaces. The city sewers will be expanded to improve water drainage. Most importantly, more trees and gardens will be planted to absorb the rain.

2010, the glacier-covered Eyjafjallajokull (AY-uh-fyat-luh-YOE-kuutl-uh) volcano erupted in southern Iceland. Lava flowed out. Westerly winds carried volcanic ash across much of Europe. Airports throughout the continent had to close. In Iceland, the eruption quickly melted ice from Eyjafjallajokull's glacier. Flooding occurred in nearby towns and farm fields. Lava destroyed nearby property. The ash made it hard for people and animals to breathe. But lava also enriches the soil. Within a few years, crops again covered the ground.

Wonders in the Night Sky

From Iceland to northern Russia, people experience several weeks of White Nights each summer. This happens because the Sun does not set until after midnight and then rises again in a few hours. During the winter, those lands experience a long period with no sunlight during the day.

During winter nights, the northern sky puts on a light show. A curtain of blue, green, purple, or red light swirls in the night sky. This amazing sight is called the aurora borealis (northern lights). It is caused by particles in solar winds that have been caught in Earth's magnetic field.

FOUR

A CHANGING NATURAL ENVIRONMENT

Reindeer graze on the tundra on one of Norway's Svalbard Islands.

Nature and people have made many changes to Europe's land and bodies of water. In turn, those changes have affected the habitats of the continent's plants and animals. Today, about 15 percent of Europe's animal species are endangered.

Thawing Tundra

Land along most of Europe's Arctic Coast is covered with **tundra**. Because this land is frozen most of the year, trees do not grow there. The frozen soil is called **permafrost**. In the summer, the top several inches (cm) of permafrost thaw. Wildflowers and small shrubs bloom during days

Saving Seeds in Svalbard

Deep inside a mountain on one of Norway's Svalbard Islands is the Svalbard Global Seed Vault. The vault is beneath 400 feet (122 m) of permafrost. It contains seeds from almost one million different food crops from all over the world. To preserve the seeds, the vault's temperature is kept at -4°F (-20°C). The seeds are being preserved in case of a major regional or global disaster. If all the world's crops were destroyed, farmers could plant seeds from Svalbard.

with almost twenty-four hours of sunshine. Mosses, lichens, ferns, and grasses also grow on the tundra. They provide food for the tundra's large reindeer herds. In the winter, reindeer find those plants under the snow. Arctic hares, caribou, lemmings, and birds also feed on tundra plants. Arctic foxes feed on hares; snowy owls, on lemmings; and wolves, on caribou. Polar bears live far north in the tundra. They venture out on Arctic ice to feast on the ocean's seals.

Climate change has brought warmer temperatures and a different kind of precipitation to the tundra and the Arctic Ocean. Winter storms sometimes bring freezing rain instead of snow. Reindeer cannot chop through the ice-covered ground to reach mosses and other food. This causes the herd to decrease. Warmer summer temperatures now attract large flocks of geese to the tundra. They are overgrazing the tundra's grasses. As the grasses disappear, desertification is taking place. With warming, polar bears have less Arctic ice to walk on. This limits their hunting area.

Falling Forests

About 66 percent of Europe's forests have been cut down. Through hundreds of years, forestland became farmland, mining areas, or cities. Logging in today's forests produces paper and lumber for building homes and making furniture.

Still, forests stand throughout much of northern Russia and in Germany's Black Forest. The northern forests have fir, Scotch pine, and Norway spruce trees. Brown bear, elk, and moose make homes among those trees. Farther south, forests of ash, beech, poplar, and willow trees stand. Owls and woodpeckers live in those trees. Gray wolves and deer are the main large animals. Forested mountains of Southern Europe provide homes for endangered Alpine ibex, Iberian lynx, Alpine marmots, and chamois.

Along the Mediterranean Sea, small forests of Aleppo pine, cypress, holm oak, and evergreen cork oak grow. The outer layer of bark from cork oaks is stripped off carefully, flattened, and dried. A new outer layer then forms. The cork is used to make bottle stoppers, mats, and tiles.

Białowieża Forest

Białowieża Forest is on the border between Belarus and Poland. This forest dates back to 8000 BCE. It is the last of Europe's original forest areas. At one time, the kings of Poland owned the forest. Since 1979, a large part of the forest has been protected as a United Nations Educational, Scientific and Cultural Organization (UNESCO) World Heritage Site. Visitors may only enter the forest with a guide. They move through the forest on foot or in a small horse-drawn cart. Motorized vehicles are not allowed.

Alder, ash, beech, birch, giant oak, Norway maple, Norway spruce, and Scotch pine trees fill the forest. Several species of eagles, owls, and storks roost in the trees. Otters, beavers, and cranes make homes in the forest's wetlands. Endangered mammals such as European bison, elk, wild boar, lynx, and wolf are protected in this forest. Boar feast on acorns dropped from the oak trees.

Fewer Grasslands

Camargue horses live only in the marshland of southern France.

From central Hungary through Ukraine to Russia, steppe covers the land. This dry land has short grasses and small shrubs but few trees. Saiga antelope once grazed on the grasses. Because most of the steppe's grasses have been plowed under, saigas are almost extinct. The land now produces large crops of corn, sugar beets, sunflower seeds, and wheat.

Sometimes the steppe goes through long droughts. Then the crops die and the land turns to dust. In some parts of the steppe, farmers are turning the land back to grasses. Now they are raising cattle and sheep on the steppe.

The Camargue is marshy grassland. It covers the Rhone delta in southern France. Reeds, orchids, and meadow flowers grow there. White horses and black bulls run wild in the Camargue. Much of this area has been drained to raise rice, fruits, and vegetables. Now the wild animals have less room to roam.

Changing Life on Lakes, Rivers, and Coastlines

Europe's lakes, rivers, and coastlines provide homes for many fish, birds, and other wildlife. Many of those waters have become polluted. Oil leaking from nearby wells and pipelines has polluted the world's largest lake—the Caspian Sea. Sturgeons that once filled the lake are now endangered.

This lake in Greece has polluted water that threatens the egret, other wildlife, and humans.

Many of the rivers, including the Danube, Rhine, and Volga, are also polluted. Waste products from farms, cities, and factories foul the rivers. Now, fewer ducks, geese, and white swans can live along Europe's riverbanks. When the rivers reach the sea, their pollutants also harm coastal plants and animals.

Europe's oceans and seas are full of fish and shellfish. Atlantic herring, Atlantic mackerel, Atlantic salmon, blue whiting, cod, and haddock are the main species in cold, northern waters. Oysters, octopus, squid, and Mediterranean mussels live in the warmer southern seas. Overfishing along Europe's coasts has decreased the number and types of fish. Scientists think that Bluefin tuna will become extinct in the Mediterranean by 2050. About 25 percent of Europe's marine mammals are also endangered. They include the harp seal and three species of whales.

FIVE

PEOPLE AND CHANGE

Europe's mild climate and rich soil for growing food crops has made this continent a good place for people to live. Currently, Europe has the world's third-largest population. Only Asia and Africa have larger populations. About 736 million people live in Europe—11 percent of the world's population. Europe's largest country is Germany with about 81 million people. Vatican City, within the city of Rome, Italy, has the world's smallest population—about 800 people.

Changes in Population Growth

Europe has the world's slowest-growing population. By 2050, the continent's population might decrease to 565 million people. Europe is the only continent where the population is expected to decrease. Eastern Europe's population is expected to decrease the most. Of

Many people work in Vatican City, but few live there.

course, some countries, such as France, Ireland, Spain, and the United Kingdom, expect their populations to grow. Most of the increase will occur from immigration. Each year, thousands of people move to those four countries from other European countries and from nearby African and Asian countries.

The main reasons for Europe's decreasing growth are a low birthrate and emigration. A low birthrate has occurred because European couples are having fewer children. Most Europeans graduate from high school. Many go to college. Then, they establish their careers before getting married and having children. Also, large numbers of Europeans emigrated to find better jobs. Many Europeans moved to North America, South America, and Australia. A few others have made homes in nearby countries in Africa and Asia.

Several countries, including Germany, Italy, and Russia, encourage people to have more children. Overall though, many Europeans think that a smaller population will be good for the environment. With fewer people, less demand will be put on Europe's land and water resources. More land could again be covered with forests and grasses. Europeans might even slow the effects of climate change.

The Sami — An Endangered People

About 70,000 Sami live in far northern Finland, Norway, Russia, and Sweden. They are Europe's only native people. They have lived in the cold, snowy lands for several thousand years. The Sami live in harmony with the natural environment by herding reindeer. They eat their meat, drink their milk, and use their skins for clothing. Long ago, Sami lived in tents made of reindeer skins. Now, they live in modern houses with television and the Internet. Some Sami still use reindeer to pull sleds and wagons. Most Sami now use snowmobiles or ATVs (all-terrain vehicles) for transportation.

Today, less than 25,000 Sami speak their native languages. At school, they use the main language of the country in which they live. Some Sami languages are already extinct. When people lose their language, they usually also lose their culture. They become more like the people whose language they have adopted. This has already happened to other small ethnic groups in Europe.

Where Europe's People Live

Most of Europe's people live in river valleys and along the coasts. Those areas have the best farmland or harbors for fishing boats. River valleys and coasts are also where all of Europe's large cities were built. Europe's largest cities are Moscow, Russia; London, England; St. Petersburg, Russia; Berlin, Germany; and Madrid, Spain.

Around one-fifth of the people in the United Kingdom live in small villages, such as this one on the far southwestern coast.

Europe has the world's fourth-largest urban population. About 73 percent of Europeans live in cities. Individual European countries have even larger percentages of city dwellers. Most of them are in Northern and Western Europe. The tiny countries of Monaco and Vatican City are 100 percent urban. Belgium, Malta, San Marino, and Iceland are more than 90 percent urban. Europe's cities have good schools and companies that provide well-paying jobs. That is why so many people live in them. By 2030, about 85 percent of Europe's people will be living in cities.

Moscow, Russia — Europe's Largest City

FIELD TRIP EXPLORATION

Moscow is both the capital of Russia and Europe's largest city. About 8 million people live in Moscow. In 1147, the city was founded as a fortress on the Moscow River. Today, this fortress is known as the Kremlin. Within the Kremlin's walls are beautiful old churches, cathedrals, and palaces. The headquarters of Russia's government are also in the Kremlin.

Moscow is one of the few cities in Europe with a growing population. Since 2002, the city's number of new residents has risen at a rate of about 200,000 each year. Many of them come from nearby Asian countries. Moscow is also one of the few European cities with plans to expand. Government leaders want to double Moscow's land size. Most government offices and offices of large companies will move to the new part of the city. The move will relieve traffic near the center of the city. To achieve this plan, large areas of forestland will be cut down. Many Russians oppose this plan, but the government owns the forests.

In Southern Europe, the olive harvest begins in late fall and continues through the winter.

The other 27 percent of Europe's population live in rural areas. In some countries, that percentage is much higher. For example, about 85 percent of the people in Liechtenstein live in rural areas. Some of these people raise sheep and cows on grassy mountain slopes.

Other highly rural areas are in Eastern Europe. For example, more than 50 percent of the people in Bosnia-Herzegovina, Moldova, and Slovenia live in rural areas. In those countries, farming continues to be an important way to make a living. In other parts of Europe, fewer people are needed on farms. Those farms use mechanical equipment to plant, weed, and harvest crops. Some of Europe's rural population also live in fishing villages. This is especially true in coastal areas of Northern Europe.

More of Europe's people will continue to live in cities rather than in rural areas. However, the number of people living in Europe's cities is decreasing as Europe's overall population decreases. Some cities already have many empty apartments. Leaders in some of Germany's cities are making plans for a future with less people. They are tearing down old buildings and replacing them with parks and trees.

SIX

LOOKING FOR SOLUTIONS TO PRESENT-DAY PROBLEMS

Europe is the only continent facing a future with fewer people. This could be a problem. It could also have a positive outcome for Europe's natural environment and climate change.

Europe's Major Problems

One of Europe's main problems is a lack of well-paying jobs for its highly educated population. This problem has caused many Europeans to move to other continents. With a decreased population, Europe has fewer young people to support the aging population. A European's average life expectancy is now 78 years. Already, more Europeans are in the over-65 age group than in the under-15 age group.

Although the permanent population is decreasing, the number of tourists is increasing. In recent years, about 500 million people have visited Europe annually from other continents. In warm weather, sunny

Europe is also rich in natural resources. The continent has some of the world's richest soil. It produces some of the world's largest amounts of barley, oats, potatoes, rye, sugar beets, and wheat. Olive groves and vineyards in Southern Europe lead the world in olive and grape production. By 2080, the amount of Europe's food crops is expected to increase by at least 15 percent. Today, less mining takes place in Europe. Still, about 30 percent of the world's coal and large amounts of iron ore are mined in Eastern Europe. Northern Europe is a major producer of oil and natural gas.

Europe also has important sources of natural, clean energy. Iceland and Italy use geothermal power as a source for electricity. That power comes from heat generated underground near active volcanoes. Throughout Europe, hydroelectric power is generated by dams on the continent's rivers. Wind farms with wind turbines—modern-day windmills—are located offshore or on land in places with strong, steady winds. Today, wind turbines generate about 20 percent of Denmark's electricity.

Since the 1950s, several European governments have worked together to improve life in Europe. Today, twenty-seven countries belong to the European Union (EU). Among other issues, the EU is working to restore Europe's natural environments. It has established policies to protect Europe's tundra, forests, and coastlines. It has set up programs to improve Europe's air and water quality. All of those actions, plus a decreasing population, should greatly improve Europe's environment.

GLOSSARY

canal	a deep ditch or channel dug on land that connects bodies of water and that allows for barge and ship traffic
chlorofluorocarbons	chemicals used as coolants in refrigerators and air conditioners and as propellants in aerosol sprays
climate change	an increase or decrease in temperature or rainfall over a long period of time
continent	a large land mass
deforestation	cutting down of entire forests
desertification	weakening of soil from deforestation, drought, overuse of land, or climate change
drought	a long period of time with little or no rainfall

glacier	a large sheet of slowly moving ice and snow
habitat	the natural place in which a plant or animal lives
open-pit mine	a huge hole dug by miners and from which minerals are removed from the ground
permafrost	land that is permanently frozen beneath the surface
steppe	dry, treeless land covered with thick grasses
tectonic plates	the hard sheets of moving rock that make up the earth's crust
tundra	cold, dry, treeless land near the Arctic Ocean

FIND OUT MORE

BOOKS

Ganeri, Anita. *Europe's Most Amazing Animals*. Animal Top Tens. Chicago: Heinemann-Raintree, 2008.

Miller, Gary. *The Rhine: Europe's River Highway*. Rivers Around the World. New York: Crabtree Publishing Company, 2010.

Peppas, Lynn. *The Alps*. Mountains Around the World. New York: Crabtree Publishing Company, 2011.

Royston, Angela and Michael Scott. *Europe's Most Amazing Plants*. Plant Top Tens. Chicago: Heinemann-Raintree, 2008.

Woods, Michael. *Seven Natural Wonders of Europe*. Seven Wonders. Minneapolis: Twenty-First Century Books, 2009.

Woodward, John. *Climate Change*. Eyewitness Books. New York: DK Publishing, 2008.

WEBSITES

Europa—Kids Corner
http://europa.eu/kids-corner/index_en.htm
Play games, work puzzles, and take quizzes to learn more about this continent.

Europe Weather
http://weather.org/europe.htm
This page shows current weather conditions across Europe, with links to the weather in each European country.

INDEX

Page numbers in **boldface** are illustrations.

ABOUT THE AUTHOR

Patricia K. Kummer has a B.A. in history from St. Catherine University in St. Paul, Minnesota, and an M.A. in history from Marquette University in Milwaukee, Wisconsin. She has written chapters for several world history and American history textbooks and has authored more than sixty books about countries, states, natural wonders, inventions, and other topics. Books she has written for Cavendish Square include *Working Horses* in the Horses! series and the seven books in the Climates and Continents series.